Prehistoric Life

Ramona-Ann Gale

Macdonald/Educational

Managing Editor Chris Milsome
Editor Verity Weston
Assistant Editor Carol Woolley
Design and Research Sarah Tyzack
Production Philip Hughes

First published 1973
Reprinted 1974
Macdonald Educational
49 Poland Street
London W1A 2LG

contents

ISBN 0 356 04344 4

Printed in Great Britain by
Morrison and Gibb Ltd, London and Edinburgh

The beginning of life a chemical soup

Creation of the earth

Men have imagined many stories about the creation of life, but the story science tells is stranger than any myth. Scientists are generally agreed on three points: the earth was first made up of gases, then these became liquid and the earth became smaller.

But when did this spinning globe of glowing gas become recognizable as our earth and able to support life? The origin of the earth and the beginning of life are inseparable. To follow one story is to discover the other.

The earth cools down

The glowing globe of gas cooled to a liquid stage. Then the surface of the earth cooled to form a solid crust of rock around the core. Clouds formed and it rained for centuries. At first the rain drops fell on to the hot rocks, sizzled and were gone. They were instantly evaporated.

Slowly the rocks cooled. When their temperature dropped below the boiling point of water, the rain began to flow over the rocks, soaking up chemicals, and collecting in pools.

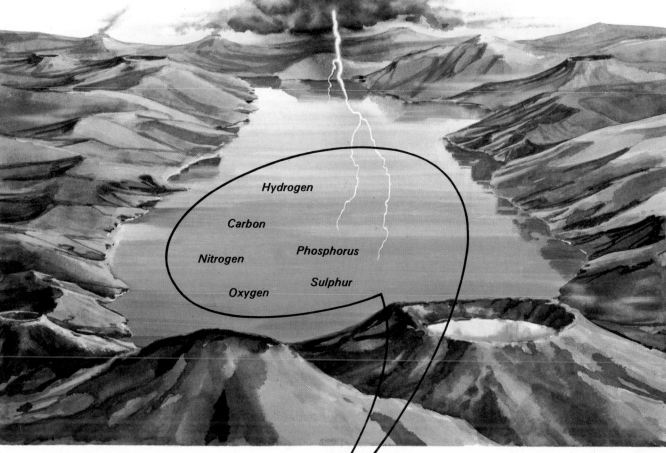

Hydrogen

Carbon

Nitrogen

Phosphorus

Oxygen

Sulphur

▲ The pools of water made by the first rain contained all the chemicals necessary for life. The most important chemicals are listed on the illustration. It may have been a charge of electricity from a bolt of lightning that caused these chemicals to react in such a way that they became the first living substance.

A living cell

◀ Scientists reckon that it took about 1,800 million years from the creation of the earth for the first living cell to evolve from the "chemical soup".

It took just under twice that time for a simple one-celled form of life to evolve into the mass of millions of different kinds of cells that make a human being.

Life in the sea

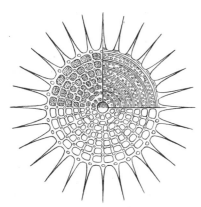

▲ This is one type of Radiolarian. It is so small in real life that you could not see it with the naked eye.

Radiolarians belong to the group Protozoa (single-celled animals). They have existed in the seas in vast numbers since the Cambrian period, nearly 600 million years ago.

Today, there are over 400 species of these microscopic creatures and many of them are similar to those from earlier periods.

▲ These examples of Radiolarians
▼ have very different forms.

The delicate external skeleton of a Radiolarian is mostly made of a mineral called silica which is extracted from the sea water.

Radiolarians are so abundant that over the millions of years countless dead ones have sunk to the bottom of the sea. They form millions of square miles of ooze in the oceans today.

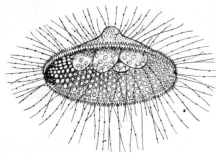

The first plants and animals

The life forms that developed out of the "chemical soup" were simple organisms, able to live off chemicals in the primitive mud. These first organisms were plants because only plants can make their food directly from the chemicals in the environment.

Organisms which did not make their own food but ate plants developed later and were the first animals. The first plants were algae and the first single-celled animals were the Protozoa.

Gradually, single-celled animals joined together to form colonies. Cells in the colonies began to specialize: some cells only caught food while others only digested it. A colony of cells began to behave like a single animal. Thus, over a period of 2,000 million years, living creatures with many cells evolved.

By the time of the Ordovician period, 500 million years ago, the land was still lifeless but the life of the seas was vast. Some of its forms are illustrated below. Some animals, such as the jelly-fish and the sponges, were soft-bodied. Others, such as the trilobite and giant nautiloid, had developed hard, protective shells for self-defence.

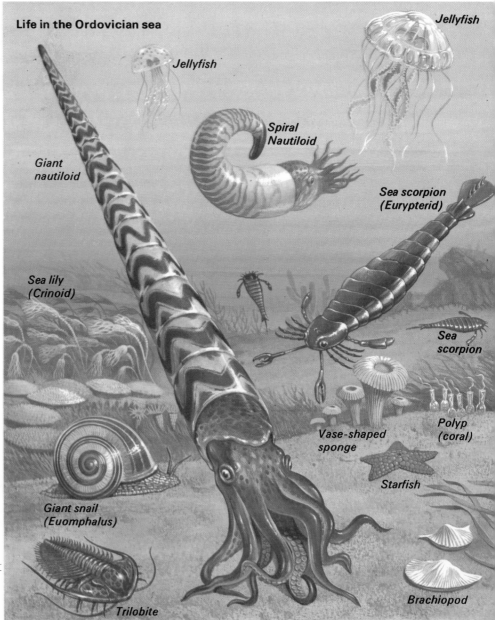

Life in the Ordovician sea

Jellyfish

Jellyfish

Giant nautiloid

Spiral Nautiloid

Sea scorpion (Eurypterid)

Sea lily (Crinoid)

Sea scorpion

Vase-shaped sponge

Polyp (coral)

Giant snail (Euomphalus)

Starfish

Trilobite

Brachiopod

Fishes: the first vertebrates

Vertebrates are animals which have backbones. The first vertebrates were armoured fish-like animals. They appeared in the sea during the Ordovician and Devonian periods.

Pteraspis and *Anglaspis* in the picture below were early armoured fishes. They had no jaws to bite with; their mouths were just small holes or slits and they wiggled along the bottom of streams and lakes, sucking algae and other vegetable food out of the mud.

Bothriolepis was also a very primitive fish, but it showed two important developments. It evolved jaws and paired fins. Jaws allowed *Bothriolepis* to leave its mud-grubbing life at the bottom of the stream. It could search for and seize larger prey. The fins on each side of the body helped to stabilize the fish, greatly improving its swimming skill.

Cheirolepis had fins with thin ray-like bones. Many modern fish have this type of ray fin, and scientists believe that fishes like *Cheirolepis* may be the ancestors of most species of fish living today.

Dipterus was a primitive lungfish. If there was a drought and the pond or river where it lived dried up, *Dipterus* could survive because, in addition to its gills, it had lungs with which it could breathe air.

Eusthenopteron was a member of an important group of fish species from which the first land vertebrates evolved. *Eusthenopteron* had lobe fins which may have been strong enough to support it on land. This lobe fin contained the supporting bones from which the limb bones of the first amphibians developed.

▲ Like prehistoric lungfish such as *Dipterus,* the modern lungfish can live in water and on land. In a dry season it can make a mud cocoon and lie asleep in it. Here, scientists have persuaded the lungfish to make its cocoon in a tin can in order to move it easily from one place to another.

▲ The lungfish is removed from the tin and its cocoon. When the lungfish is in its cocoon, it is in a condition of reduced activity called aestivation. It lives off its muscle and lies with its tail over its eyes to prevent loss of moisture.

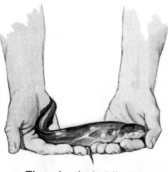

▲ The scientist holding the lungfish is about to put it in water. It still wears a leather-like cocoon it made around itself in the drying mud. When this soaks off the lungfish will start its normal activities again. Lungfish can live four years out of water.

Armoured fishes

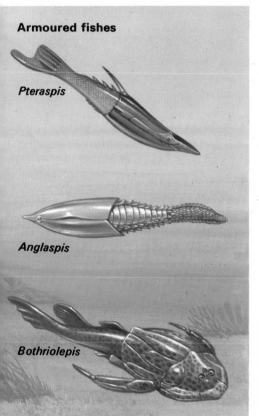

Pteraspis

Anglaspis

Bothriolepis

Devonian fishes

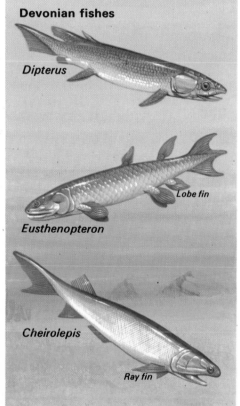

Dipterus

Eusthenopteron

Lobe fin

Cheirolepis

Ray fin

Duncleosteus was a huge carnivorous fish of the Devonian period, often called the Age of Fishes. *Duncleosteus* could be about 35 feet (10 m.) long.

Duncleosteus

Life invades the land amphibians

A trace of green scum

By the end of the Silurian period the sea was surging with life but the land was still dead. Then traces of green scum began to appear along the shore.

Plants spread from the water and established themselves across the plains. Now several small creatures, probably insects, ventured onto the land. Fishes may then have become the first vertebrates to invade the land. There they found an abundant food supply in the form of insects.

Fishes breathe with gills and swim with fins. To leave the water, they had to adapt to breathing air and find a new way of moving about.

During the Devonian period there were often droughts and the freshwater streams dried up. In order to survive, some freshwater fishes evolved lungs to breathe air and their fins became adapted to manoeuvring their bodies across dry land in search of water. The first steps on land were taken by fin not foot. Thus our distant ancestor emerged from his watery world.

In the picture above a lobe-finned fish crawls along the shore. From creatures like this the amphibians very slowly evolved.

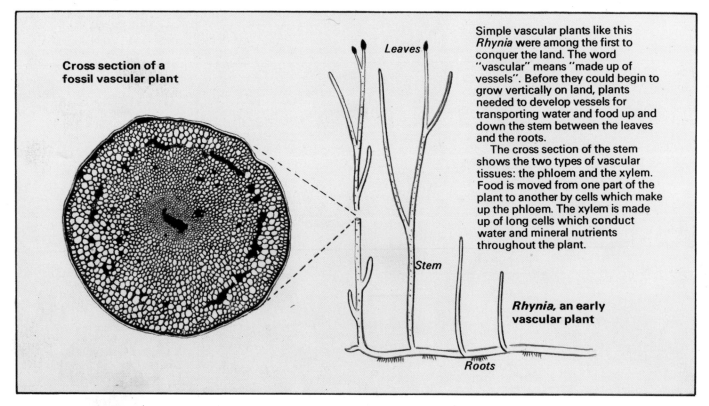

Cross section of a fossil vascular plant

Leaves

Stem

Roots

Rhynia, an early vascular plant

Simple vascular plants like this *Rhynia* were among the first to conquer the land. The word "vascular" means "made up of vessels". Before they could begin to grow vertically on land, plants needed to develop vessels for transporting water and food up and down the stem between the leaves and the roots.

The cross section of the stem shows the two types of vascular tissues: the phloem and the xylem. Food is moved from one part of the plant to another by cells which make up the phloem. The xylem is made up of long cells which conduct water and mineral nutrients throughout the plant.

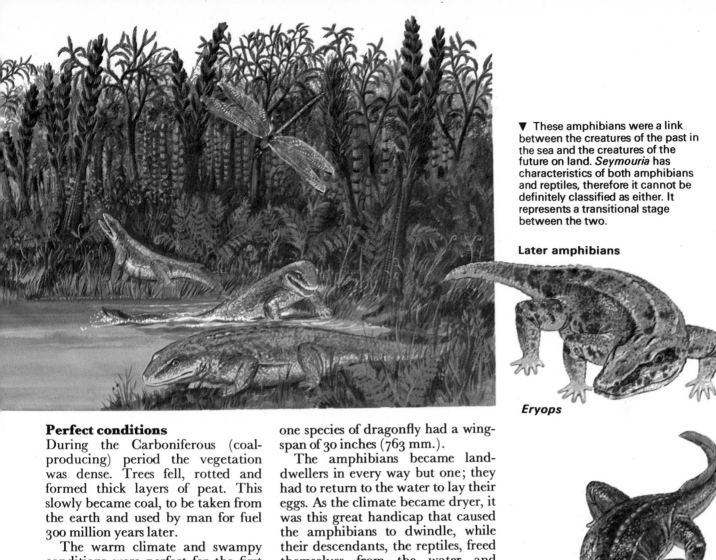

▼ These amphibians were a link between the creatures of the past in the sea and the creatures of the future on land. *Seymouria* has characteristics of both amphibians and reptiles, therefore it cannot be definitely classified as either. It represents a transitional stage between the two.

Later amphibians

Eryops

Perfect conditions

During the Carboniferous (coal-producing) period the vegetation was dense. Trees fell, rotted and formed thick layers of peat. This slowly became coal, to be taken from the earth and used by man for fuel 300 million years later.

The warm climate and swampy conditions were perfect for the first amphibians and also for the insects; one species of dragonfly had a wing-span of 30 inches (763 mm.).

The amphibians became land-dwellers in every way but one; they had to return to the water to lay their eggs. As the climate became dryer, it was this great handicap that caused the amphibians to dwindle, while their descendants, the reptiles, freed themselves from the water and flourished.

Diplocaulus

Seymouria

Paracyclotosaurus

Life cycle of a frog

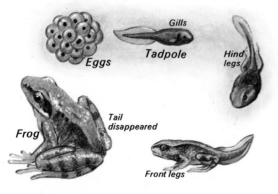

Eggs

Gills

Tadpole

Hind legs

Tail disappeared

Frog

Front legs

◄ The double life of an amphibian is illustrated by the life-cycle of the modern frog. Frogs' eggs are laid in water. Fish-like tadpoles with gills hatch, grow, develop lungs and limbs and leave the water to live on land.

► The salamander which is also an amphibian has the long body of the typical fish. The legs stick out from the sides, so that it moves along on its stomach in a series of s-shaped twists which resemble those of a swimming fish.

Reptiles everywhere

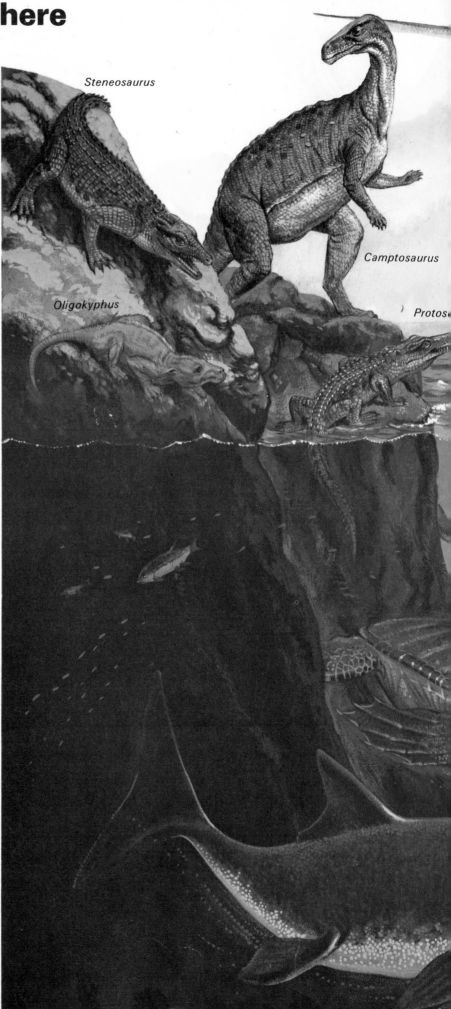

Steneosaurus

Camptosaurus

Oligokyphus

Protos

World dominion

For over 150 million years reptiles dominated the world. A description of the Mesozoic Era, the Age of Reptiles, reads like an advertisement for a science fiction film. The land was ruled by mighty monsters, the sky filled with flying dragons and the oceans infested with sea-serpents.

Reptiles were far better adapted to life on land than the amphibians. A covering of scales stopped the reptilian skin drying out. Instead of sticking out at the side of the body, reptile legs were under it, supporting it and making movement on land more efficient. The biggest amphibian problem that reptiles solved was the inability to reproduce away from water.

The amniote egg

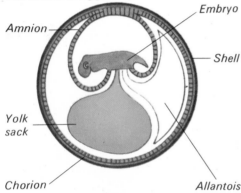

Amnion

Embryo

Shell

Yolk sack

Chorion

Allantois

A solution is found

The reptiles successfully freed themselves from the water while the amphibians remained tied to it forever. This was because reptile and amphibian embryos, or unborn babies, could not survive being unprotected from the air. So the amphibians continued to lay their eggs in water but the reptiles gradually developed a special kind of egg. This is known as the amniote egg.

Here, the embryo could develop in its own private pool protected by a leathery shell. Inside the amniotic sac the creature could pass through the tadpole stage and develop into a land animal before birth.

The shell prevented the egg from drying out and the yolk supplied the growing embryo with food. A tadpole obtains oxygen from the surrounding water and excretes waste into the water. Inside the amniote egg the allantois provides these services.

Pteranodon

Rhamphorhynchus

Kronosaurus

Elasmosaurus

Archelon

Tylosaurus

Ichthyosaurus

Rhamphorhynchus probably lived on the cliffs above the sea and swooped down to catch fish. Its fearsome jaws contained forward-pointing, long, sharp teeth which made a very efficient fish trap. Its long tail, which was used as a rudder in flight, ended in a diamond-shaped membrane. The wing was a thin membrane supported only by the elongated fourth finger.

Pteranodon, with a wing span of 25 feet (7.6 m.), was the largest flying animal of all time.

Protosuchus is the oldest known crocodile ancestor. Its 3 foot (0.9 m.) length was protected by solid bony plates. _Steneosaurus_ was another crocodile whose skull alone was 3 feet (0.9 m.) long.

Oligokyphus did not look like a reptile because it had mammal-like features including the hairy covering and the way its legs were positioned. _Oligokyphus_ was another step on the ladder of evolution which led to the mammals.

Camptosaurus was an early plant-eating dinosaur.

A fundamental law of nature is that evolution does not work backwards. Sea reptiles could not simply shed their feet and once again grow fins like their ancestors, the fish. They had to adapt their land limbs to work efficiently in water.

The ichthyosaur looked so much like a fish that it is difficult to believe it was not. But the bone structure beneath the skin was that of a reptile. This reptile did the only sensible thing in adapting to its environment: it evolved a stream-lined fish shape.

Modern reptiles

Today the surviving reptiles are represented by three main groups: tortoises and turtles, snakes and lizards, and crocodiles.

Sea turtle

▲ The distant ancestor of the sea turtle is the 12 foot (3.6 m.) long _Archelon_ seen on the left.

Land tortoise

▲ The land tortoise has survived since the Jurassic period.

Boa constrictor

▲ Snakes are descended from lizards that moved by swaying from side to side.

Estranne crocodile

▲ Crocodiles still have long hind legs and short front ones as their extinct dinosaur cousins did.

Conquest of the air

▶ The length of the fingers and toes of *Hypsilophodon foxi* suggest it could have lived in the trees. It may have been an ancestor of the first birds.

Hypsilophodon foxi

▶ The wing membrane might have developed as an aid to jumping or gliding from branch to branch.

▼ In a ground-dwelling reptile the wing might have developed as an aid to running. At speed the reptile could take off and glide.

Flying reptiles

The first creatures to fly were insects, followed much later by reptiles and the first feathered birds.

The flying reptiles made three basic changes. They developed a wing membrane which was supported by a very long fourth finger and stretched to the thigh. Then their skeletons became lighter and stronger and the part of their brain which controlled vision and movement grew larger.

The reptiles' primitive wings were unable to flap up and down like a bird's wings. The flying reptiles had to glide, using the wind and air currents. But even though they flew clumsily, the fact that they were able to fly gave them several advantages. The flying reptiles were able to escape enemies, to spread their species over a wider area and to catch food.

Reptiles in fancy dress

Although flying reptiles lived for 100 million years, they did not evolve sufficiently to survive and they became extinct at the end of the Mesozoic Era. Birds, the most efficient flying vertebrates, inherited the sky.

The earliest known bird-like creature is *Archaeopteryx*. It kept many reptilian characteristics. It had teeth in its primitive beak and claws at the end of its wings. It has been described as a reptile in a fancy dress feather costume. But even the feathers can be traced to a reptilian origin as they are made up of exactly the same chemicals as the horny scales of reptiles.

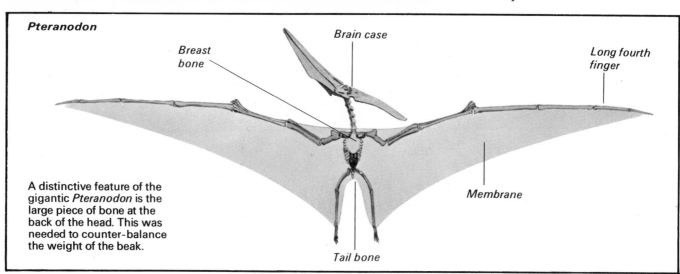

Pteranodon

Breast bone

Brain case

Long fourth finger

Membrane

Tail bone

A distinctive feature of the gigantic *Pteranodon* is the large piece of bone at the back of the head. This was needed to counter-balance the weight of the beak.

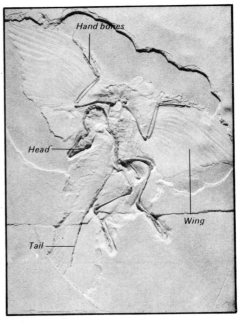

◄ *Archaeopteryx,* the first bird, shows a mixture of reptilian and bird-like features. It had bird feet and feathers but reptilian teeth, tail, and claws on its wings.

Hand bones

Head

Wing

Tail

▲ If it had not been for the clear feather markings, this Archaeopteryx fossil from the Jurassic period would have been classified as a reptile.

The skeleton of an *Archaeopteryx*

The skeleton of a modern pigeon

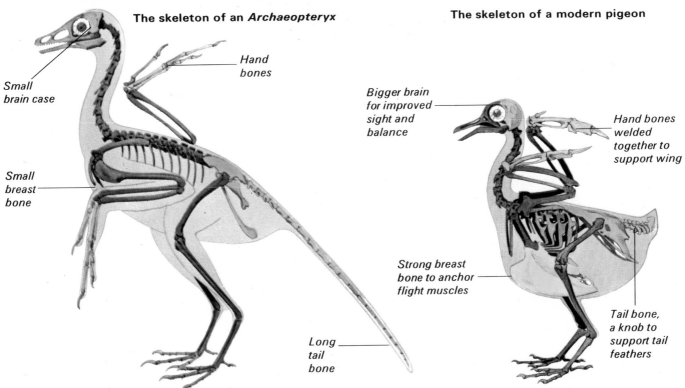

Hand bones

Small brain case

Small breast bone

Long tail bone

Bigger brain for improved sight and balance

Hand bones welded together to support wing

Strong breast bone to anchor flight muscles

Tail bone, a knob to support tail feathers

▲ Comparison of the body structure of *Archaeopteryx* with that of the modern bird shows how the bird has evolved and successfully adapted to its aerial existence.

▲ The body of the modern pigeon makes it very efficient at flying. Modern birds have spread to every kind of environment and they are highly successful.

Dinosaurs rule the earth

Terrible reptile

The Age of Reptiles lasted for about 150 million years. The best known life forms in this successful reign were the dinosaurs. The dinosaurs are probably the most misunderstood of the pre-historic animals. Not all the dinosaurs were huge and ferocious. Some were small and harmless.

This false impression goes back to when dinosaurs were first named. The word "dinosaur" is based on two Greek words: "deinos" meaning huge or terrible and "sauros" meaning lizard or reptile.

At the time the group was named, only a few of the larger dinosaurs were known, so "huge reptile" seemed a good name. By the time smaller forms were discovered the name dinosaur was in common use so its meaning "terrible reptile" was applied to these creatures too.

As more dinosaurs were discovered scientists divided them into classes according to their origin, bone structure or feeding habits. The five groups here show how many different types of dinosaurs developed during their long period of dominance.

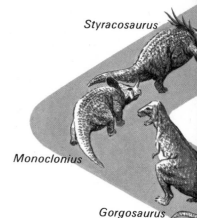

Styracosaurus

Monoclonius

Gorgosaurus

There are many dinosaur fossils of the late Jurassic period. As giants require food and space, these fossils indicate a world with plentiful vegetation and vast areas of open space.

▶ This parade of the dinosaurs through the ages shows how much they changed. From the beginning they were specialized, well adapted reptiles. One of the most striking features of the fossil record is the world-wide distribution of the dinosaurs.

Brontosaurus

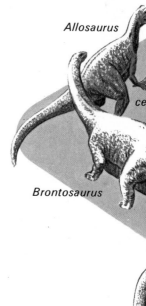

Allosaurus

Prote ceratop.

Brontosaurus

Brachiosaurus

The nasal crests on this group of duck-billed dinosaurs suggest they fed in the water but the contents of their stomachs show they ate land plants. They used their duck-bills for stripping trees.

Lambeosaurus

Corythosaurus

200 million years ago

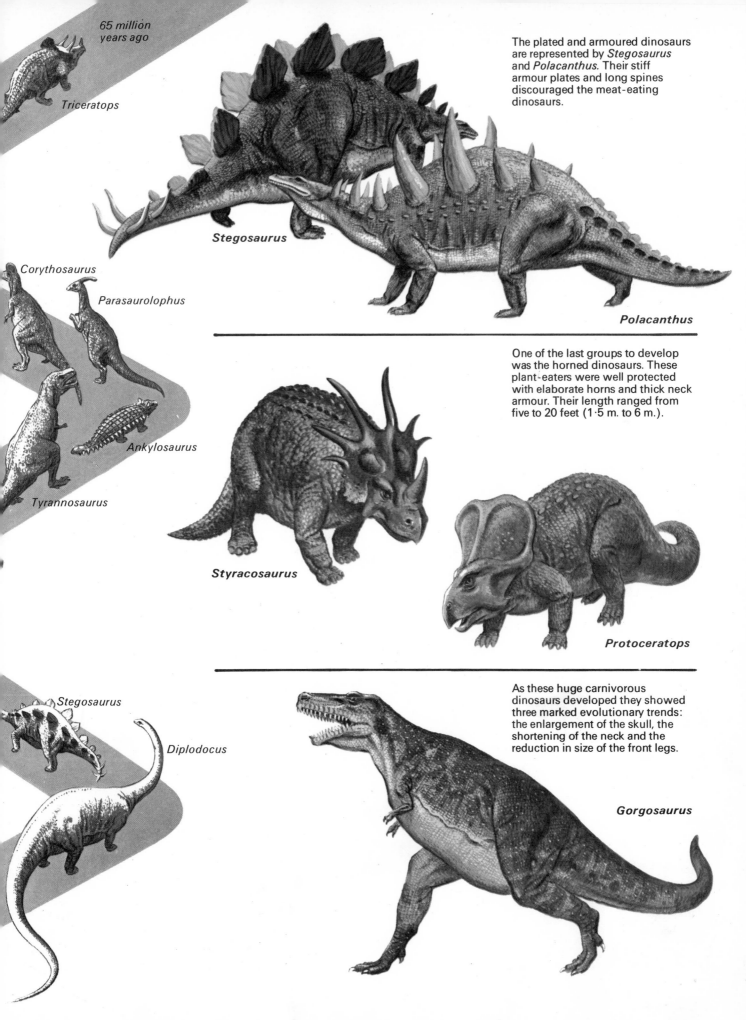

Triceratops

The plated and armoured dinosaurs are represented by *Stegosaurus* and *Polacanthus.* Their stiff armour plates and long spines discouraged the meat-eating dinosaurs.

Stegosaurus

Corythosaurus

Parasaurolophus

Polacanthus

Ankylosaurus

Tyrannosaurus

One of the last groups to develop was the horned dinosaurs. These plant-eaters were well protected with elaborate horns and thick neck armour. Their length ranged from five to 20 feet (1·5 m. to 6 m.).

Styracosaurus

Protoceratops

Stegosaurus

Diplodocus

As these huge carnivorous dinosaurs developed they showed three marked evolutionary trends: the enlargement of the skull, the shortening of the neck and the reduction in size of the front legs.

Gorgosaurus

13

Fight to the death

A hungry meat-eating dinosaur, *Tyrannosaurus,* attacks a plant-eater, *Triceratops,* which desperately defends itself with its great horns. *Tyrannosaurus* was the biggest two-legged dinosaur that ever lived. From head to tail it was 40 feet (12 m.) long, and it carried its huge vicious head 17 feet (5 m.) above the ground.

Some early mammals, *Triconodons,* are taking advantage of the fight and eating *Triceratops'* eggs. On the right *Anatosaurus* watches the fight and in the background are a group of *Ornitholestes.*

New plants inhabit the land

In the early Cretaceous period changes took place in plant life. Flowering plants spread and the jungles of primitive trees faded. Together with flowers came modern insects to pollinate them.

The success and expansion of the flowering plants provided a new food source. Some scientists believe that the spread of the new plant life caused the dramatic increase in the number of plant-eating dinosaurs. Plant-eaters such as *Triceratops* would have needed a vast amount of food to survive.

Dinosaurs, like other reptiles, are believed to have been cold-blooded. This meant that they needed a long spell of rest and cooling off after a short burst of activity during which their body temperatures increased. For that reason a fight would have to be short and decisive.

If dinosaurs lived today . . .

▲ It is very difficult to imagine the size of dinosaurs from the distant past. By putting them into familiar settings their sizes can be compared with everyday sights. If it were alive today *Brontosaurus*, would enjoy a bath in the canal where the water would support part of its great 40 ton (40½ tonne) weight.

► *Procompsognathus* does not fit most people's idea of what a dinosaur should look like. It was not much bigger than a turkey and ran along quickly on long slim legs. It was one of the early meat-eating dinosaurs. Perhaps today it would beg a tit-bit from a tourist on the quay side.

◀ *Ankylosaurus* was well equipped to deal with modern-day traffic. Its tank-like body was more than a match for any Mini. Long spikes would assure its right of way on any pedestrian crossing. The club-like tail would settle any disputes over a parking place.

◀ If seen today by a passing motorist, *Ornitholestes* might well be mistaken for an ostrich with hands. The body shape, long neck, small head and horny beak indicate that it must have lived like the large ground-dwelling birds of today. But unlike them, *Ornitholestes* could use its hands to catch small creatures.

▼ *Tyrannosaurus rex* was probably the most ferocious meat-eater of all time. The wide-gaping jaws contained six-inch (152 mm.) long sharp teeth, well adapted to biting and tearing its prey. He was not the sort of companion you would welcome to a lunch-time picnic by the sea. You would more than likely be on his menu.

Dead end why did dinosaurs die out?

The dinosaurs were a very successful species which survived for 150 million years. This page shows some of the ways in which dinosaurs were well-adapted to their environment. Why then did they die out?

The great mystery

The dinosaurs adapted themselves to live successfully at sea, on land and in the air. They were many and varied and were found all over the world.

With other great reptiles such as the ichthyosaurs, the dinosaurs flourished for 150 million years. Why did they become extinct?

At the end of the Cretaceous period virtually all the dinosaurs in all parts of the world were wiped out. This seems to indicate that something drastic happened. But fossil records show no evidence of sudden changes in plant life, climate or physical surroundings.

The Rocky Mountains rose up at the end of the Cretaceous period and caused the swamps where many of the plant-eating dinosaurs lived to dry up. This mountain building had, however, been going on for millions of years, so there is no reason to suppose that it suddenly caused a whole group of reptiles to disappear.

Some experts think that the climate which might have become cooler in the Cretaceous period, could have killed the dinosaurs. We know that the dinosaurs were cold-blooded and could not adjust to extreme changes of temperature. But this change of temperature on land would not explain why the ichthyosaurs in the sea became extinct as well, because water temperature changes very little.

Two brains or one?

▶ This poem about *Stegosaurus* was written by an American, Bert Taylor, and was first printed in the *Chicago Tribune*.

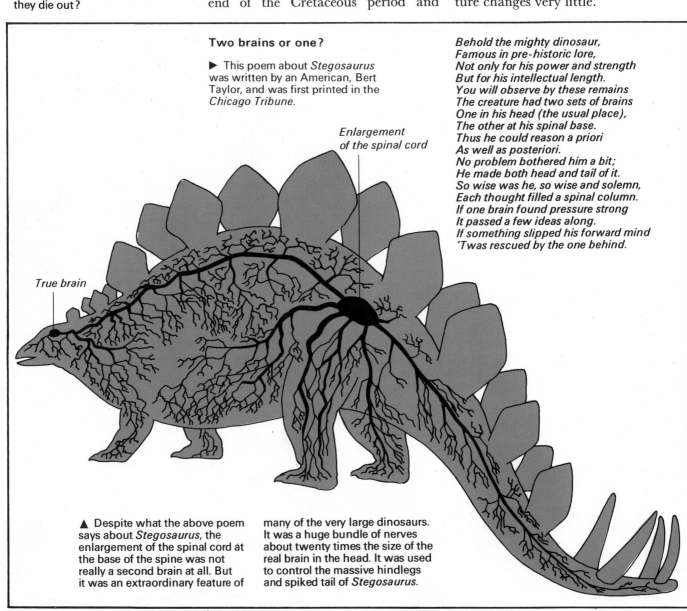

Enlargement of the spinal cord

True brain

Behold the mighty dinosaur,
Famous in pre-historic lore,
Not only for his power and strength
But for his intellectual length.
You will observe by these remains
The creature had two sets of brains
One in his head (the usual place),
The other at his spinal base.
Thus he could reason a priori
As well as posteriori.
No problem bothered him a bit;
He made both head and tail of it.
So wise was he, so wise and solemn,
Each thought filled a spinal column.
If one brain found pressure strong
It passed a few ideas along.
If something slipped his forward mind
'Twas rescued by the one behind.

▲ Despite what the above poem says about *Stegosaurus*, the enlargement of the spinal cord at the base of the spine was not really a second brain at all. But it was an extraordinary feature of many of the very large dinosaurs. It was a huge bundle of nerves about twenty times the size of the real brain in the head. It was used to control the massive hindlegs and spiked tail of *Stegosaurus*.

Local extinctions

Of course the world changed and this seems a good theory to explain the disappearance of the dinosaurs until you come across a creature like the turtle. It has had the same structure since the Jurassic period, yet the unchanging turtle has done very well in a changing world. Other theories for dinosaur extinction include epidemics of disease and radiation from an explosion in outer space.

Perhaps dinosaur extinction was not a world-wide catastrophe, but a series of local extinctions with different causes happening over a long period of time. For example if the plant-eaters died out in one place the meat-eaters would have nothing to prey on and would die out as well.

The extinction of the dinosaurs is important because it left the world empty for the mammals. Why it happened remains a mystery.

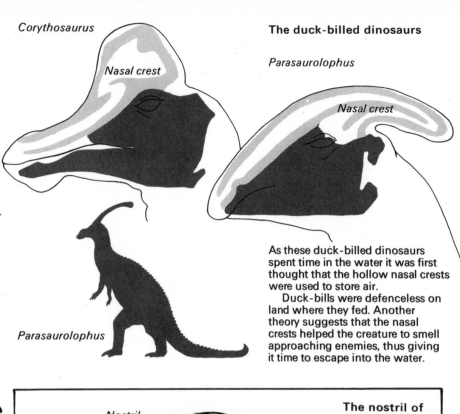

Corythosaurus

Nasal crest

Parasaurolophus

The duck-billed dinosaurs

Parasaurolophus

Nasal crest

As these duck-billed dinosaurs spent time in the water it was first thought that the hollow nasal crests were used to store air.

Duck-bills were defenceless on land where they fed. Another theory suggests that the nasal crests helped the creature to smell approaching enemies, thus giving it time to escape into the water.

The forelimbs of *Ornitholestes*

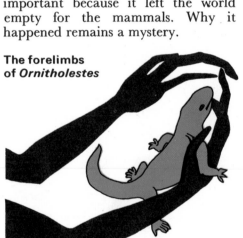

▲ Usually when forelimbs developed, they were for use in moving along. But the forelimbs of *Ornitholestes* became larger in order to grasp prey.

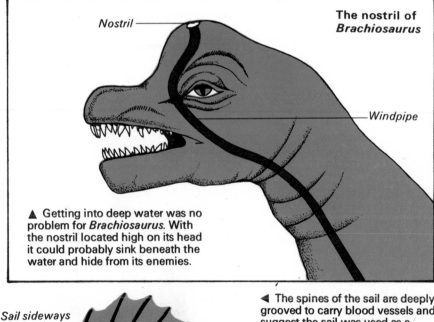

Nostril

The nostril of *Brachiosaurus*

Windpipe

▲ Getting into deep water was no problem for *Brachiosaurus*. With the nostril located high on its head it could probably sink beneath the water and hide from its enemies.

Sail faces the sun = heat loss

Sail sideways to the sun = heat gain

◄ The spines of the sail are deeply grooved to carry blood vessels and suggest the sail was used as a temperature regulator. By turning the sail to the sun, *Dimetrodon* was warmed up. It could catch prey before other reptiles of a similar size were active.

Mammals take over

Tetonius

Diatryma

Hyrachus

Uintatherium

Moeritherium

Miacis

Hyracotherium

A new environment

The Eocene period, the first Age of Mammals, started 60 million years ago. The mild damp climate encouraged the growth of sub-tropical jungles and forests. Flowering plants and deciduous trees spread. Many plant-eating mammals developed specially tough teeth for grinding this abundant food supply.

The first primates, the highest order of mammals, were living in the trees, like *Tetonius* in the picture. Bats, the only mammals capable of true flight, also first appeared at this time.

A giant bird

As the bats were nocturnal, or active at night, they were not in direct competition with the birds which were active during the day. Some birds did not fly at all. On the ground strutted the seven foot (2 m.) tall *Diatryma*.

This dangerous creature was carnivorous and a threat to small mammals such as *Hyracotherium*. Although it was only the size of a fox terrier, *Hyracotherium* should have a slightly familiar look as it was the ancestor of one of the mammals which still exist today.

Mammals everywhere

The ancestors of three other well-known modern mammals appeared during the Eocene period. A quick "spot the ancestor" quiz would give the following answers: *Hyracotherium* was an early horse, *Miacis* an early cat, *Moeritherium* an ancestor of the elephant family and *Hyrachus* an ancestor of the rhinoceros.

Mammals did not only occupy the land and air. In the Eocene oceans there were sea mammals such as sea cows, whales and porpoises. Reptiles no longer ruled the earth. The mammals had taken over.

Alti-camelus

Nesodon

Baluchitherium

Proconsul

Dinohyus

Merychippus

Deinotherium

Proconsul

Merychippus

Room to roam
The Miocene period started 25 million years ago and lasted 14 million years. The climate was cooler and vegetation changed. Forests and jungle gave way to open plains.

The Golden Age of Mammals began with the spread of grass over the prairies. In a world of dense forest and woodland, animals could not move about on the ground at any great speed. But now the wide open prairies provided space to roam and run. Small hooves gradually grew bigger and the first swiftly running mammals evolved.

The first horses
Hyracotherium had four toes on each of its front feet and was only one-third of the size of *Merychippus*, its Miocene descendant. *Merychippus* had only three toes and when it ran its weight was carried on the larger and stronger middle toe.

Pliohippus, not illustrated here, was a later type of horse ancestor and had only one main toe on each foot. The modern horse also has only one main toe, its hoof.

Deinotherium was a Miocene elephant. Unlike the modern elephant, its tusks grew from the lower jaw.

Man's Miocene ancestor
Man may have evolved from a group of Miocene creatures like *Proconsul*. As the forest disappeared, perhaps *Proconsul* was forced to leave the safety of the trees and become the first primate to experiment with life on the ground.

Baluchitherium was probably one of the largest land mammals of all time. It looked at its world through eyes which were 25 feet (7.6 m.) from the ground. *Baluchitherium*'s height was an advantage; it ate leaves that small animals such as *Dinohyus* could not reach.

The great Ice Age mammals adapt

▶ The family tree of the elephant is interesting because it shows how the animal adapted itself to different environments. Modern elephants have shorter necks than their ancestors. Because of this, the mouth could not reach the ground and food was taken in by the upper lip which lengthened into a strong muscular trunk.

The evolution of the elephant

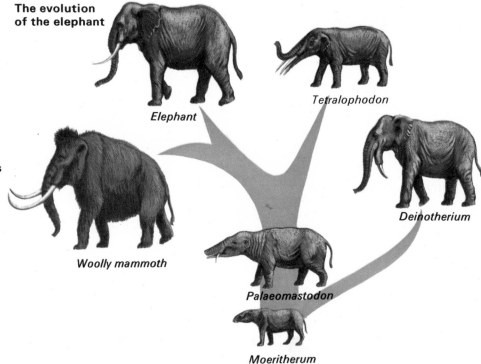

Elephant

Tetralophodon

Deinotherium

Woolly mammoth

Palaeomastodon

Moeritherum

Distribution of elephant species in the Pleistocene epoch

▲ During the Pleistocene epoch (about 100,000 to 20,000 years ago) elephants were far more widespread than now. The map shows that they lived in many different parts of the world.

Distribution of elephants today

▲ This map shows the parts of the world in which elephants are found today.

Explosive evolution

"Explosive evolution" is the term used to describe the rapid development of mammals and their adaptation to various habitats or natural surroundings. The variety of forms shows how successful they were.

During the reign of the reptiles the mammals remained small and insignificant. It was to their advantage to do so because they were living in a world dominated by carnivorous dinosaurs.

But when the dinosaurs left the scene the mammals were well equipped to take over. They were warm-blooded which meant that they were active for longer periods than the cold-blooded reptiles. Mammal limbs were better adapted to movement; their senses of smell and hearing were also better and their covering of hair kept them warm when the climate became cooler.

With few exceptions mammals developed the placental form of reproduction. This meant that the embryo was kept inside the mother's body until it was born alive. Unlike reptiles, mammals cared for and fed their young.

Possibly the most important development was in the brain. With mammals came the first signs of the use and advantages of brain power.

◀ An early stage in mammal development is shown by the duck-billed platypus which still lays eggs. This type of mammal probably exists today for two reasons: it lives in an isolated part of the world and does not have to compete for food with other groups.

▶ The opossum is a member of another minor group of mammals, the marsupials. At birth, the tiny baby crawls up the mother's body and into the pouch where it feeds until sufficiently developed to come out. Other marsupials are kangaroos and wombats.

Reindeer

Woolly rhinoceros

Cave bear

Polar fox

Musk oxen

At the end of the Pliocene period the climate became much colder. Ice sheets spread out from the North and South Poles. Glaciers built up high in the mountains. Slowly the huge ice masses slid down the mountains, crept over the plains and covered a quarter of the continents. Plants and animals either adapted to the harsh climate or retreated south.

However, the Ice Age was not one long frozen winter. It was broken by warmer periods when the glaciers retreated.

Many scientists believe we are now living in a warm period of the Great Ice Age and that glaciers will return.

Woolly mammoth

Man appears

▶ These pictures give an impression of the way fossil evidence suggests man could have evolved.

Proconsul *Ramapithecus* *Australopithecus*

Man emerges

There is no one simple explanation of the evolutionary changes that have produced modern man. Working from the fossil evidence available, scientists can draw certain conclusions. New fossil finds sometimes make it necessary to change these conclusions. However, most scientists agree that there is a basic outline to man's evolution.

The evolutionary changes seem to begin with changes in the feet, legs, pelvis and lower part of the back bone. This brought man upright so he could walk on two legs. As they were no longer needed for moving along, the shoulders, arms and hands were free to develop manual skills.

Development of the brain

Finally the teeth and jaws decreased in size and the brain increased. The development of the brain came last. These evolutionary changes took place separately at different times but each new skill helped others to develop.

There are people who point to the lack of fossil evidence of intermediate forms of man and say that man did not evolve slowly over millions of years. They suggest that spacemen from other planets landed on earth, selected and interbred with the local primitive population and humanized them in a comparatively few years.

The evidence for this interesting theory is too long and complicated to include here. However, the fact that the theory exists illustrates one of the features that set prehistoric man apart from the other animals: his ability to think creatively.

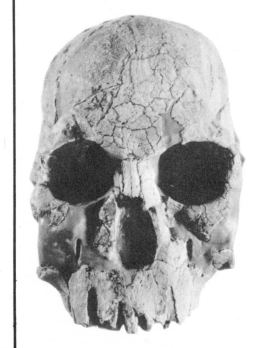

Earliest known man

In November, 1972 Richard Leakey made a startling announcement. He had found a fossil which was "almost certainly the oldest complete skull of early man", estimated at 2.6 million years old.

The skull was pieced together from fragments found near Lake Rudolf, Kenya. Until this find the earliest man fossils were thought to be one million years old.

The Leakey skull is different from other skulls of early man and it goes against modern theories of the evolution of man. For this man is a million years older than *Australopithecus,* the next oldest man, yet has a brain twice the size.

Fossil head reconstruction

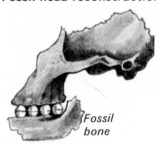
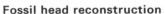
Fossil bone

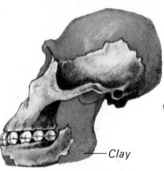
Clay

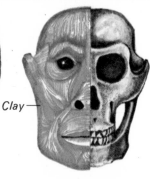
Clay

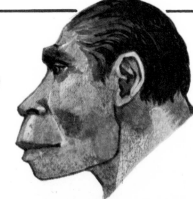

▲ To reconstruct a fossil the original pieces of fossil bone must first be fitted together like a three-dimensional jigsaw puzzle.

▲ The next step is when an experienced sculptor, using clay, carefully adds to the shape of the skull indicated by the fossil bones.

▲ Muscle markings on the original bone show the sculptor where thicker clay should be added to form the layers of deep muscle.

▲ More clay is added to form ears, chin, tip of the nose and skin covering. The hair and skin colour must be left to the sculptor's imagination.

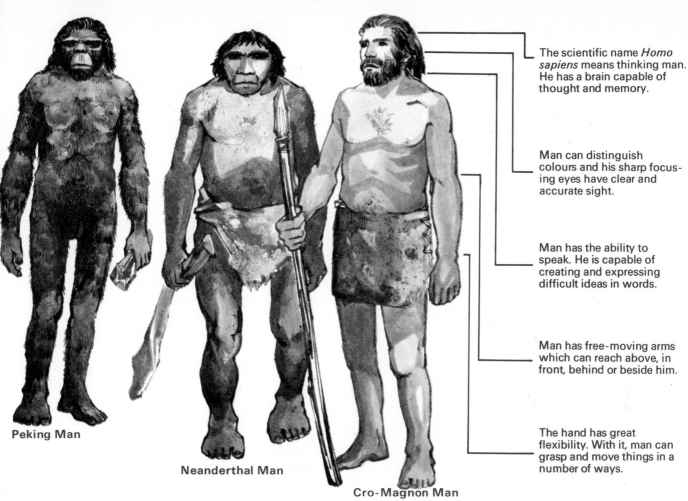

Peking Man

Neanderthal Man

Cro-Magnon Man

The scientific name *Homo sapiens* means thinking man. He has a brain capable of thought and memory.

Man can distinguish colours and his sharp focusing eyes have clear and accurate sight.

Man has the ability to speak. He is capable of creating and expressing difficult ideas in words.

Man has free-moving arms which can reach above, in front, behind or beside him.

The hand has great flexibility. With it, man can grasp and move things in a number of ways.

▲ Peking man lived 222,000 years ago. He lived in caves, made tools, hunted and used fire.

▲ Neanderthal man was related to modern man. He may have invented religion and war.

▲ Cro-Magnon man is modern man. He took over from the *Neanderthals* 35,000 years ago.

Chimpanzee

Homo erectus

Modern man

Brain

Eyebrow ridge

Heavy jaw

Large canine teeth

Brain

Eyebrow ridge

Heavy jaw

Brain

Chin

Comparison of the skulls shows that as the primate brain gets bigger, the face area gets smaller. The shape of prehistoric man's brain can be seen by making a cast of the inside of the skull. By studying this cast scientists have guessed that *Homo erectus* could see as well as we can but could not use his hands or speak as well.

Hunters and gatherers

Mere guesswork

The bones of prehistoric man give us an idea of what he looked like and how he evolved. The weapons and tools found with the bones give us a clue to his way of life. But of some things there is no fossil record. No-one knows when man began to speak, when he first lived in tribes, or when he became a hunter.

The best that scientists can do is to use the clues they have and give a general outline of the probable way in which man's culture developed through the ages.

Everyone for himself

For man's ancestors it was everyone for himself. The food was probably abundant and literally only an arm's length away. But when man's ancestors descended from the trees, it was a bit different. Food was not abundant. So why they left the trees is the question that remains to be answered.

It was a period of climatic change and the great forests were reduced in size. Better adapted tree-dwellers such as the apes might have driven man's ancestors out on to the plains.

At one time everyone was a foodgatherer. But when larger groups were formed food gathering became the job of the women and children.

A digging stick was woman's most valuable tool. With this she could dig out edible roots and tubers and also kill small animals.

Man stands up

So man's ancestors climbed down and stood up. It has been suggested that the upright position was developed so he could see more clearly across the plains he was now to inhabit. But there are other theories.

One expert suggested the aquatic theory. He said that when man's ancestors abandoned life in the trees, those who took to the dry hot plains of the Pleistocene period soon died.

The ones that survived were the ones that took to the water. There, the upright position would mean they could wade out into the water far enough to be safe from their enemies. It has recently been suggested that it was woman's idea to take to the water.

Carrying a child she was unable to run away from any danger she might meet on land. The water proved a very safe refuge for her and the shoreline was literally crawling with a plentiful food supply. She stayed, and of course man followed. The small family unit was the first group of people to be formed.

The first larger group man formed was probably the hunting group. Unfortunately most people have a mistaken idea about man, the hunter. The hunters all too frequently came home empty handed. This meant that the woman, the foodgatherer, was the main provider for the family.

It is estimated that women provided 60-80 per cent of the food eaten by the family. This figure is borne out by tribes who still live by the food-gathering and hunting way of life.

People could only live in large groups in an area which had enough food for them all.

Big animals were the obvious source of food but hunting needed good weapons and intelligent organization and co-operation. Here a group of men are killing a reindeer with spears.

Tools and weapons

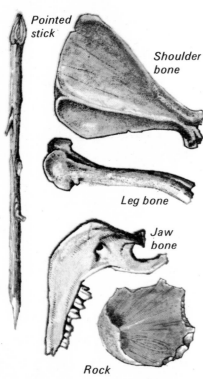

Pointed stick

Shoulder bone

Leg bone

Jaw bone

Rock

▲ The first tools were things that came easily to hand such as sticks and stones and animal bones. Teeth, tusks and femur bones of extinct gazelles, pigs and antelopes have been found with some *Australopithecus* fossils. These might have been used as tools for scraping, cutting and chopping.

Making tools

Man develops skills

At first man did not make tools. He simply picked up what was handy when he needed it and threw it away afterwards. Some scientists say that the time when man started to make tools was the time when he took a step up from the animals. As man did not have sharp teeth and fangs like the other animals he needed a cutting tool.

The earliest man-made tool was probably a very simple cutting tool like the stone chopper. A round stone was chosen and three or four chips knocked off to give a cutting edge. The sharp edge was easily broken, so the working life of the tool was only a few days. This probably explains why so many samples of this type of pebble tool have been found.

As the pictures below show, tools became gradually more sophisticated. The fact that hand-axe styles were the same over wide areas and for long periods of time suggests two things: that the skills were handed on from father to son, and that meetings must have taken place between neighbouring groups.

Fire was perhaps the most exciting and dangerous new tool that early man learned to use and make. Until man used fire, he was little more than an animal with tools and weapons instead of claws. Man used fire for four main purposes: to warm himself, to protect himself from wild animals, as a centre for the tribe to gather round after dark, and for cooking.

Some experts have suggested that cooking helped to change man from an animal to a human being more effectively than anything else. Cooking made the food softer to eat, and greatly reduced the amount of time spent in eating. The time he saved could be spent on developing other skills. Fire was the key tool. It made man an efficient animal.

The evolution of tools

These simple stone choppers were made by *Australopithecus* at least a million years ago. They come from Olduvai Gorge in Tanzania.

Peking man made these hand axes 220,000 years ago. He was a more skilled tool-maker than his predecessor, *Australopithecus*.

▲ Direct percussion, using a hammer-stone to break away chips and leave a sharp edge, was probably one of the earliest ways of tool making.

▲ Indirect percussion is more advanced than direct percussion. A hammer-stone and pointed stick are used to make another tool.

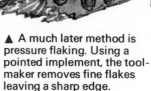

▲ A much later method is pressure flaking. Using a pointed implement, the tool-maker removes fine flakes leaving a sharp edge.

▲ Man developed the power grip (left) before the precision grip (right). As his hand became more skilful, the tools became more refined.

◄ A prehistoric man makes a tool while another makes fire by revolving a stick very fast on another piece of wood.

Making fire

▲ Fire was probably captured and used by man long before he learned to make it. Fires could have been started by lightning in forests, or could have been caused by volcanic eruptions.

When and how man first made fire is not known. He probably used the wood friction method which is illustrated above.

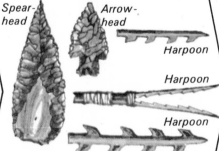

Tools like these were used by Neanderthal man, for scraping hides, 70,000 years ago.

Spear-head   Arrow-head   Harpoon   Harpoon   Harpoon

30,000 years ago Cro-Magnon man was manufacturing these elaborate finely pointed tools.

Tools for painting

Lamp   Rock paint-palette   Fur pad   feather   Shredded twig   Blow pipe

▲ When early man had learned to survive, a few people had some spare time. They had time to develop different tools: the tools of an artist.

◄ This magnificent cave painting from Lascaux, in southern France, shows the high level of skill reached by an early artist with these tools.

Mistaken identities

Woolly mammoth

Skull of the mammoth

Nasal opening

Many myths are based on the finds of large fossil bones. The myth of the one-eyed Cyclops may have been started by sailors who found large skulls in caves on the coast of Sicily.

These were mammoth skulls, but the sailors thought the large nasal opening was for the one eye of a Cyclops giant.

Cyclops

Thunder Horse

The Oglala Sioux Indians who lived and hunted the buffalo on the great plains of North America believed in a beast called the Thunder Horse. They said that during thunderstorms these gigantic animals leaped out of the clouds and helped the Sioux by driving herds of buffalo towards them. After the storm the Thunder Horses disappeared.

Captain James Cook, a famous scout and trapper who traded with the Sioux, often heard this legend of the Thunder Horse, and was once shown a huge jaw-bone by Chief Red Cloud. Cook mentioned the legend and the bone when he met Professor Marsh, the famous palae-ontologist, in 1875.

At this time the Indians were infuriated by the invasion of their lands by gold prospectors. They were likely to kill anyone who looked like a prospector, especially if he carried a pick.

But Marsh gained their confidence and was allowed to examine the Thunder Horse bones. He identified the bones as belonging to the prehistoric animal *Brontotherium*. The Indians made him an honorary chief of their tribe.

Cave bear

Cave bear bones

Dragon

The huge bones and teeth of the Ice Age cave bear probably inspired the dragon stories in many European fairy tales.

A man named Hayn found teeth and pieces of skulls in mountain caves. He fitted them together and drew a dragon skull.

Hayn then wrote a book called *Dragon skulls of the Carpathians*. His drawings show that the bones were those of cave bears.

Mary Anning

Mary Anning was born in Dorset, and spent her life there collecting, studying and selling fossils. In an age when woman's place was in the home, Mary was unusual. She was an intelligent scholar and had long discussions with the famous scientists who visited her shop.

She was also a shrewd business woman. At 12 she arranged the sale of her ichthyosaur for £23. In 1824 she discovered a plesiosaurus and sold it for over £100. At a time when little was known of fossils, these monsters that Mary dug up caused a great stir.

Georges Cuvier

Cuvier said that animals with hoofs and horns always have the teeth of herbivores or plant-eaters, and animals with claws have meat-eating teeth. That idea, called the Law of Correlation, is well-known in zoology today.

Cuvier's one mistake was in the case of *Chalicotherium*, a mammal of the Eocene period. *Chalicotherium* looked a bit like a rhinoceros and had up to six bony swellings on its head.

Cuvier rightly identified *Chalicotherium*'s teeth as those of a plant-eater. But *Chalicotherium* had long claws on its feet which it probably used to dig up roots. It was therefore an exception to Cuvier's Law of Correlation.

Ichthyosaur skeleton

▲ Mary Anning (1799-1847) was British. She was the first professional woman fossil collector.

▲ Georges Cuvier (1769-1832) was French. He is regarded as the founder of scientific palaeontology, that is the study of ancient animals. Georges Cuvier was the first person to classify animals by their internal anatomy rather than by their outside appearance which was sometimes deceptive.

► At 12 Mary Anning made her first big fossil find, this ichthyosaur. Looking at the fossil you can see why she thought at first that it was a crocodile.

► Further fossil discoveries showed scientists what the ichthyosaur's body was really like.

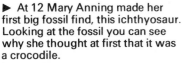

Ichthyosaur reconstruction

31

Charles Darwin and evolution

▲ Charles Darwin lived from 1809 to 1882. He was interested in natural history at an early age.

▲ This cartoon makes fun of Darwin's theories by showing him as a monkey. In fact, Darwin did not say that man descended from an ape, but that he belonged to the same branch of the family tree.

▶ The beaks of the Galapagos finches are adapted to different diets. The tool-using finch eats grubs like a woodpecker but it lacks the woodpecker's long tongue. It therefore uses a cactus spine to pick out insects from the holes it drills in the bark.

Voyage of the *Beagle*

In 1831 most people believed the biblical story that the earth was created in seven days, and that all the changes in the landscape that had happened since then were caused by catastrophes like Noah's Flood.

But a scientist, Sir Charles Lyell, believed that the earth had been created millions of years ago and that the ordinary forces of nature had caused all the changes in the landscape.

Charles Darwin was twenty three in 1831. He was offered the post of naturalist on board *H.M.S. Beagle* which was setting off on a scientific expedition round the world.

Darwin had read about Lyell's theory and been very impressed by it. During the five-year voyage he came to realize that, over millions of years, the ordinary forces of nature could have changed living things as well as the landscape.

At every stop the *Beagle* made, Darwin went ashore. He collected fossils and compared them with living species of plants and animals. He made notes of all his observations.

Finches from the Galapagos

The most significant stop was at the Galapagos Islands in the Pacific Ocean. Darwin saw that each island had its own species of finch. The species were very similar to each other except for their beaks. These were adapted to eat the different types of food available on the different islands. Darwin guessed that all these species were descended from one original species, but had evolved differently after being isolated on separate islands.

Darwin thus became convinced that living things had not always been the same, but had evolved from primitive beginnings. All living things were members of the same great family but had been forced by their changing environment to adapt and evolve.

The *Beagle* returned to England in 1836. But it was not until 1859 that Darwin published his theories in a book called *On the Origin of Species*. The book upset a great many people because it questioned the biblical story of creation, and suggested that man too was a product of evolution.

The Galapagos finches

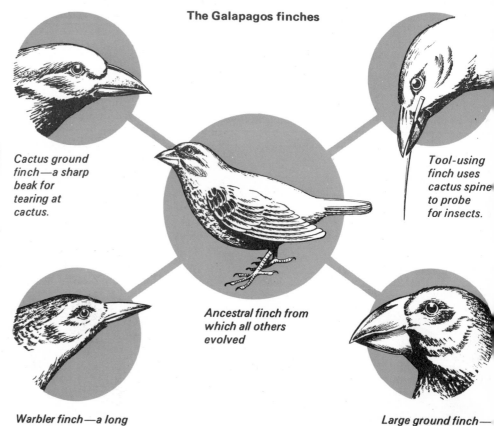

Cactus ground finch—a sharp beak for tearing at cactus.

Tool-using finch uses cactus spine to probe for insects.

Ancestral finch from which all others evolved

Warbler finch—a long sharp beak for catching insects.

Large ground finch—a strong beak for breaking open nuts.

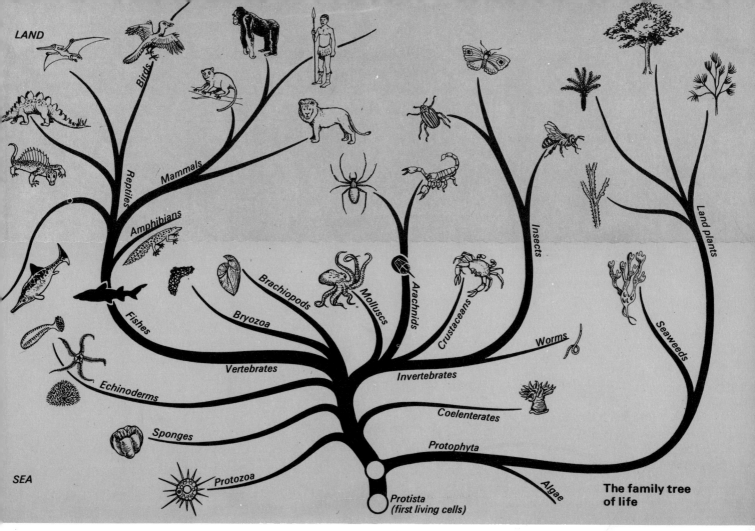

The family tree of life

LAND

Birds

Reptiles

Mammals

Amphibians

Fishes

Brachiopods

Bryozoa

Molluscs

Arachnids

Crustaceans

Insects

Land plants

Worms

Vertebrates

Invertebrates

Echinoderms

Seaweeds

Sponges

Coelenterates

Protophyta

SEA

Protozoa

Algae

Protista (first living cells)

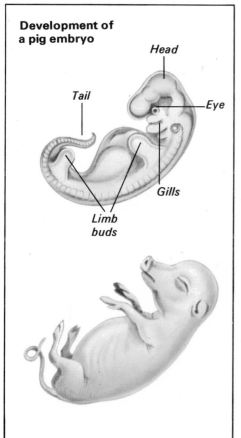

Development of a pig embryo

Head

Tail

Eye

Gills

Limb buds

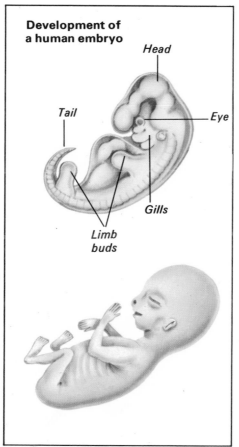

Development of a human embryo

Head

Tail

Eye

Gills

Limb buds

▲ Darwin believed that all living things are members of the same family and have developed from simple to more complex life forms. There are still many gaps in the fossil record but this family tree gives a general picture of the way life has developed and how living things are related to one another.

◄ The study of embryology also supports Darwin's theory of evolution. In spite of the differences in appearance at birth, many creatures look very much alike at the embryo stage. This suggests that they had the same ancestor.

The story in stone fossils

What is a fossil?

Fossils are the remains or traces of dead plants and animals. But not all remains of dead things are fossils; fossil remains are very old. Palaeontologists, people who study fossils, sometimes say: "If it stinks give it to the zoologist; if not, it's ours."

Most fossils are of the hard parts of animals, such as bones and shells. Usually the actual bone or shell has disappeared, but the shape and appearance is preserved.

Fossils usually form only when a dead animal is buried quickly. Much fossilization happens at the bottom of the sea where a dead creature is soon covered by sediment.

Minerals solidify

The soft parts of the animal decay leaving the skeleton. Water from the surrounding sediment fills all the tiny air spaces in the bone or shell. If the water contains a lot of minerals, these minerals slowly solidify. When solidified, the minerals keep the shape of the original skeleton.

In a different process the dead matter very very slowly dissolves and is replaced by a mineral such as silica. Fossilized wood is often made of silica.

Another sort of fossil is an imprint made in mud which has hardened into rock. In this way footprints of dinosaurs and even imprints of raindrops and fallen leaves are preserved.

Complete preservation is rare. This mammoth was overcome by cold and frozen in a block of ice.

Formation of a mould and cast fossil

A creature dies. Its soft parts decay leaving the shell. This shell is buried in the sand which hardens to rock.

Very slowly the shell material is dissolved away. But the shape or mould of the dead creature remains in the rock.

Gradually this mould is filled with fine sediments. They in turn harden and form a natural cast of the original creature.

▲ A fossil of one of the first backboned animals, the fish.

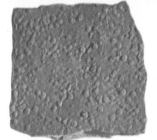

▲ The imprint of raindrops of long ago.

◄ Ripple marks are formed in shallow water and show climate.

▲ An insect caught in amber, the resin of an ancient tree.

► Coprolites, fossil excreta, tell about the diet of ancient animals.

▼ The fossilized remains of an early ape, *Oreopithecus*.

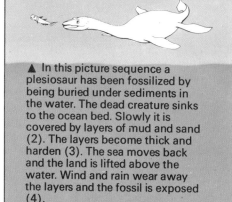

▲ In this picture sequence a plesiosaur has been fossilized by being buried under sediments in the water. The dead creature sinks to the ocean bed. Slowly it is covered by layers of mud and sand (2). The layers become thick and harden (3). The sea moves back and the land is lifted above the water. Wind and rain wear away the layers and the fossil is exposed (4).

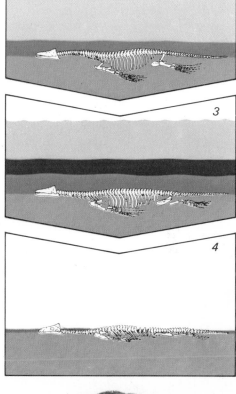

First the mould formed and acted as a container for the collected sediments which then hardened to form a cast. This made two fossils from one creature.

▲ An ammonite fossil.

▲ This swamp cypress tells us about the evolution of plants.

◄ Among the earliest known fossils is this trilobite.

How do we know? Interpreting fossils

Written in the rocks

How do we know about prehistoric life? Who can tell us and what evidence can they show to support their theories? The evidence is written in the rocks and the fossils are illustrations in the picture book of prehistoric life. But it needs a team of specialists with different skills to find, excavate, preserve and interpret these fossils.

Each expert contributes his own special piece to the jig-saw puzzle. The detailed knowledge needed on a prehistoric dig is too much for any one person to have. So the findings of the team of experts are analyzed and combined to form a complete report. It may take years to put together and judge the importance of all the material from a single site.

▲ 1. A workman has uncovered something unusual. It looks like a valuable fossil. The company calls a halt to work and notifies a team of specialists. Two of the first men to arrive on the site are the geologist and the photographer.

▲ 2. A tent is erected over the find to protect it from the weather. The geologist studies the rock in which the fossil is buried. The photographer records the work in progress as other members of the team arrive.

▲ 4. Dr Beverley Halstead, a palaeontologist, examines the find on the site at Fletton, in England.

▲ 5. A detailed record of the bones must be kept. Each one is numbered for identification purposes. The accuracy of the work done later in the laboratory depends to a great extent on the care taken in the field.

▲ 6. It is an exciting moment when the whole fossil can be seen and identified as a *Cryptoclidus* of the plesiosaur group of marine reptiles. The largest specimens in this group measure between 40 and 50 feet (12 m. and 15 m.) long.

▲ The plesiosaurus had paddle-like flippers, a thick body and short tail. The flippers were used like oars to row it through the water. Some plesiosaurs looked rather like a snake that had been pulled through the body of a turtle.

▲ 3. The palaeontologist and the preparator work carefully, uncovering the bones with picks and brushes. The palaeontologist has identified the find as a plesiosaur, a marine reptile from the Upper Jurassic period.

▲ The preparator's job is to protect and preserve the bones. A draughtsman records the exact position of all finds and notes their relationship to each other. His work is particularly important if bones have been scattered.

In the laboratory

Only one part of the work is done on the site; the other part is done in the laboratory. Palaeobotanists work on fossil plants, palaeobiologists on animal fossils. They slowly build up a picture of prehistoric plant and animal life. The geochemist and geophysicist conduct laboratory tests to find out the age of the material found at the site.

Laboratory specialists also include a petrologist who is an expert on classification of different kinds of rocks, and a pedologist who is an expert on soil and its chemical composition. There are still many gaps in the fossil record of prehistoric life but each new site and every team of specialists gives us a better understanding of the animals and plants that lived long ago.

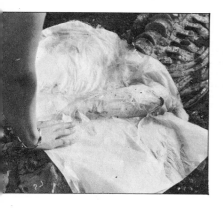

▲ 7. The small bones have been labelled and lifted. Now the preparator must deal with the larger bones. First they are covered with tissue paper which is dampened so it will cling to the shape of the bone.

▲ 8. Next, hessian soaked in plaster of Paris is used to bandage the bone as carefully as a doctor sets a broken bone. All the fragile plesiosaur bones can then be lifted and transported safely to the laboratory.

▲ 9. The preparator's work on the site is done. All the smaller bones are labelled and the larger bones encased in plaster. In the laboratory the plaster of Paris will be removed and the long job of cleaning the bones will begin.

◄ 10. The work of the team on the site is nearly finished. Their last job is carefully packing the bones in boxes and taking them back to the laboratory for further study. There another team will study the finds.

► 11. The last box of bones is loaded. Another gap in the fossil record has been filled. This particular plesiosaur was presented to the Natural History Museum in London by the chairman of the London Brick Company.

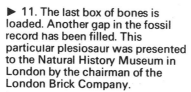

Survivors

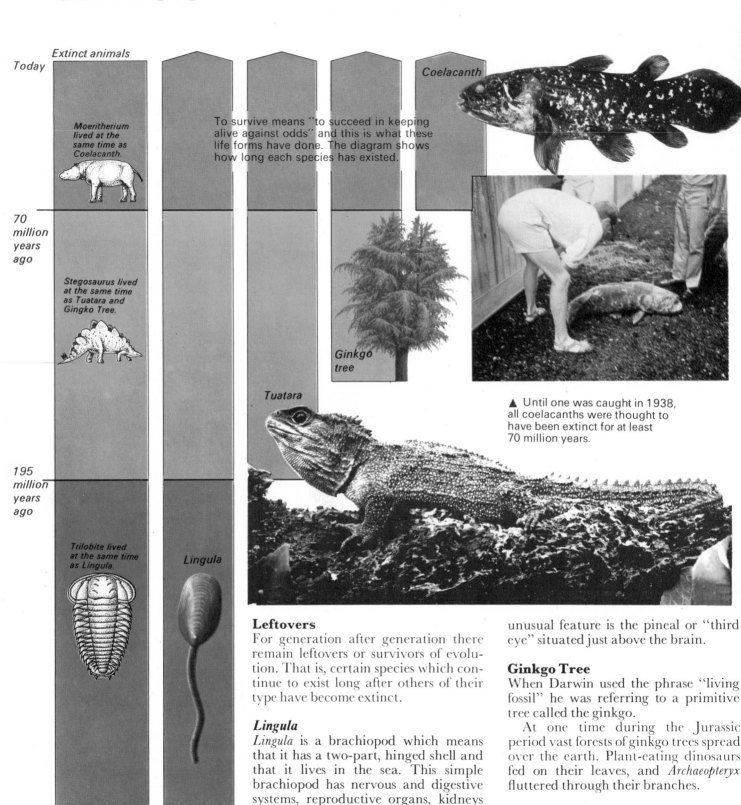

Extinct animals

Today

Moeritherium lived at the same time as Coelacanth.

70 million years ago

Stegosaurus lived at the same time as Tuatara and Gingko Tree.

195 million years ago

Trilobite lived at the same time as Lingula.

400 million years ago

To survive means "to succeed in keeping alive against odds" and this is what these life forms have done. The diagram shows how long each species has existed.

Coelacanth

Ginkgo tree

Tuatara

Lingula

▲ Until one was caught in 1938, all coelacanths were thought to have been extinct for at least 70 million years.

Leftovers

For generation after generation there remain leftovers or survivors of evolution. That is, certain species which continue to exist long after others of their type have become extinct.

Lingula

Lingula is a brachiopod which means that it has a two-part, hinged shell and that it lives in the sea. This simple brachiopod has nervous and digestive systems, reproductive organs, kidneys and strong muscles.

Tuatara

At first glance *Tuatara* looks like a modern lizard, but its skull is similar to the skulls of extinct dinosaurs. It does not have separate teeth but jagged edges on the jawbones like a beak. An unusual feature is the pineal or "third eye" situated just above the brain.

Ginkgo Tree

When Darwin used the phrase "living fossil" he was referring to a primitive tree called the ginkgo.

At one time during the Jurassic period vast forests of ginkgo trees spread over the earth. Plant-eating dinosaurs fed on their leaves, and *Archaeopteryx* fluttered through their branches.

Coelacanth

Miss M. C. Latimer discovered a coelacanth in a pile of fish brought into a South African quay by a fishing boat. It was identified and named *Latimeria chalumnae*: *Latimeria* after Miss Latimer and *chalumnae* because it was caught at the mouth of the Chalumna river.

▲ Expeditions in the Himalayas have found and photographed huge animal footprints in the snow. Explanations of these mysterious footprints range from a red bear to the Yeti. No satisfactory identification has been made. This Yeti reconstruction is based on a selection of eye-witness accounts.

Are there others?

If all these creatures survive from prehistoric times, how many others might there be which we do not know? Are there prehistoric animals still hidden beneath the oceans, high in the mountains or deep in the forests?

Is the Loch Ness Monster left over from prehistory? Countless people say they have seen a gigantic moving shape in the water. From their descriptions it sounds like a plesiosaur.

Who is the Abominable Snowman or Yeti who bounds on all fours in the Himalayan Mountains? Is he a survivor from millions of years ago?

The American Bigfoot or Sasquatch is another of these strange creatures. Might he be a relic of Neanderthal Man who still lurks unknown in the land of his modern descendants?

Identikit picture of the Yeti based on eye-witness accounts

Head and face
A long ape-like face. Ears close to the skull. Massive lower jaw; small nose with wide and flared nostrils.

Body
A powerful, hollow-looking chest, with long arms reaching to its knees and narrow, stooping shoulders.

Height
Accounts vary between slightly smaller than an average man to as much as eight feet (2.4 m.) tall.

Movement
The Yeti spends part of its time on all fours and part on two legs, somewhat like an ape or a bear.

Hair colour
Reddish brown hair forming a close fur against the body, mingling with long, hanging hairs with a grey tinge.

Hands and feet
Most witnesses describe long fingers and widely-splayed toes, with feet the size of a small man's.

How old? dates and dating

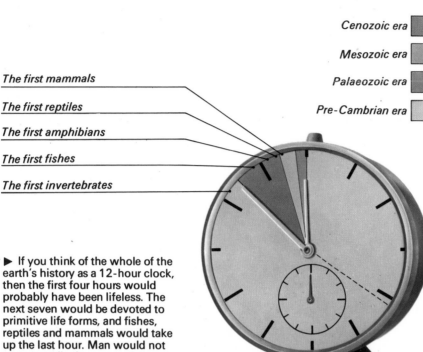

Era	PERIOD	EPOCH	
CENOZOIC		Pliocene	Land plants
		Miocene	
		Oligocene	
		Eocene	
		Palaeocene	Flowering plant
MESOZOIC	Cretaceous		
	Jurassic		
	Triassic		Fern
PALAEOZOIC	Permian		
	Carboniferous		
	Devonian		
	Silurian		Rhynia
	Ordovician		
	Cambrian		
PRE-CAMBRIAN			

- Cenozoic era
- Mesozoic era
- Palaeozoic era
- Pre-Cambrian era

The first mammals
The first reptiles
The first amphibians
The first fishes
The first invertebrates

► If you think of the whole of the earth's history as a 12-hour clock, then the first four hours would probably have been lifeless. The next seven would be devoted to primitive life forms, and fishes, reptiles and mammals would take up the last hour. Man would not appear until a few seconds to midnight.

▲ William Smith (1769-1839) is known as the "Father of British Geology". He was fascinated by stones and rock strata. He was the first person to realize that different rock formations contain different fossils, and therefore types of rock could be recognized by the fossils they contained.

Scientific methods

In 1492 the Irish Archbishop James Usher announced that he had calculated from the Bible that the earth was created at 9 a.m. on October 26th, 4004 B.C. Today, methods used for dating the earth and the fossils found in it are more scientific.

The radio carbon method of dating fossils is based on the fact that living animals take in radioactive carbon dioxide (c-14). After death the c-14 gradually changes to normal carbon (c-12). At the time of death a certain amount of c-14 is present in the body. The age of a fossil can be worked out by measuring how much c-14 is still left.

The fluorine method became famous when it was used on a famous forgery, the Piltdown man. Every bone that lies in rocks which contain fluorine slowly soaks up the fluorine. Tests on the Piltdown fossil showed that it did not contain the right amount of fluorine and could not have been as old as the hoaxers claimed.

Radioactive elements in rocks gradually break down to form lead. The age of rocks can be worked out by measuring the amount of lead in them. By using this method some geologists have estimated the age of the earth at between four and 4½ billion years.

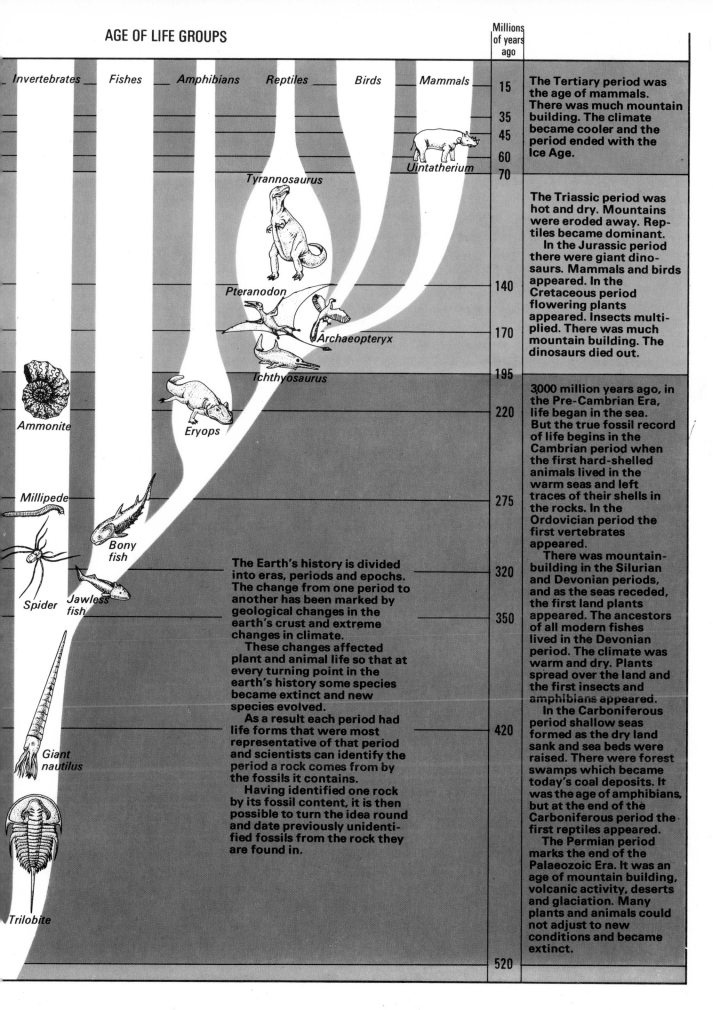

AGE OF LIFE GROUPS

Millions of years ago

Invertebrates   Fishes   Amphibians   Reptiles   Birds   Mammals

15
35
45
60
70

Uintatherium

Tyrannosaurus

Pteranodon

Archaeopteryx

Ichthyosaurus

140

170

195

Eryops

220

Ammonite

275

Millipede

Bony fish

Spider   *Jawless fish*

320

350

Giant nautilus

420

Trilobite

520

The Tertiary period was the age of mammals. There was much mountain building. The climate became cooler and the period ended with the Ice Age.

The Triassic period was hot and dry. Mountains were eroded away. Reptiles became dominant.

In the Jurassic period there were giant dinosaurs. Mammals and birds appeared. In the Cretaceous period flowering plants appeared. Insects multiplied. There was much mountain building. The dinosaurs died out.

3,000 million years ago, in the Pre-Cambrian Era, life began in the sea. But the true fossil record of life begins in the Cambrian period when the first hard-shelled animals lived in the warm seas and left traces of their shells in the rocks. In the Ordovician period the first vertebrates appeared.

There was mountain-building in the Silurian and Devonian periods, and as the seas receded, the first land plants appeared. The ancestors of all modern fishes lived in the Devonian period. The climate was warm and dry. Plants spread over the land and the first insects and amphibians appeared.

In the Carboniferous period shallow seas formed as the dry land sank and sea beds were raised. There were forest swamps which became today's coal deposits. It was the age of amphibians, but at the end of the Carboniferous period the first reptiles appeared.

The Permian period marks the end of the Palaeozoic Era. It was an age of mountain building, volcanic activity, deserts and glaciation. Many plants and animals could not adjust to new conditions and became extinct.

The Earth's history is divided into eras, periods and epochs. The change from one period to another has been marked by geological changes in the earth's crust and extreme changes in climate.

These changes affected plant and animal life so that at every turning point in the earth's history some species became extinct and new species evolved.

As a result each period had life forms that were most representative of that period and scientists can identify the period a rock comes from by the fossils it contains.

Having identified one rock by its fossil content, it is then possible to turn the idea round and date previously unidentified fossils from the rock they are found in.

Project making model dinosaurs

A *Diplodocus* skeleton

Scale models of prehistoric animals are easy to make in balsa wood. You can make skeleton models or outline shape models, all to the same scale, and set up your own tabletop museum. Let's start with a skeleton model of *Diplodocus*, which is shown (actual size) below. You will need balsa sheets of the following thicknesses: $\frac{1}{16}$ in., $\frac{1}{8}$ in, $\frac{3}{16}$ in., $\frac{3}{32}$ in. and $\frac{3}{8}$ in., and some balsa cement.

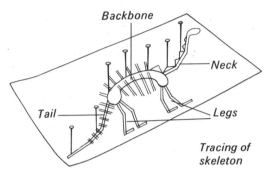

Backbone

Neck

Tail

Legs

Tracing of skeleton

First, make a tracing of the skeleton on greaseproof paper and pin it out on a flat board for working on. Make a separate tracing of the backbone and copy it on to $\frac{3}{16}$ in. sheet balsa. Cut it out carefully with a modelling knife and pin over the skeleton drawing.

To make the shape of the neck, take a 9 in. length of $\frac{1}{8}$ in. sq. balsa strip and from it cut the five neck sections according to the shape on the plan. Pin these out over the drawing and fill in each crack with

balsa cement.

The tail is made of three parts: one length of $\frac{3}{16}$ in. sq. balsa strip, a shorter length of $\frac{3}{16}$ in. × $\frac{1}{8}$ in. strip tapered to $\frac{1}{8}$ in. at one end, followed by a 6 in. length of $\frac{1}{8}$ in. sq. strip. Cement together and pin down over the drawing.

Cut the legs from $\frac{1}{8}$ in. sq. balsa and crack-bend to shape. Trace and cut two pelvis bones and two shoulder blades from $\frac{1}{16}$ in. balsa sheet. Cement the legs in place, adding one pelvis piece and one shoulder blade on top to hold secure.

Now the spine pieces can be cut to length and carefully cemented in place one by one. Trace and cut the back spines from $\frac{3}{32}$ in. sq. strip and the neck spines from $\frac{1}{16}$ in. sheet. The head parts are also cut from $\frac{1}{16}$ in. sheet. You can also add one set of ribs ($\frac{1}{16}$ in. sq. strips) at this stage. Whilst the cement is drying, cut a 6 in. × 3 in. base from $\frac{3}{8}$ in. thick balsa or ply wood and paint black.

Unpin the skeleton from the tracing. Turn it over and cement on the remaining ribs and second pelvis and shoulder blade "bones". Then cement the end of each leg to the base. You will need pins and other supports to hold the skeleton upright until the cement has set.

Outline models

As a quicker method of making prehistoric animal models you can cut out "solid" body and leg shapes from balsa sheet and then cement the legs to each side of the body. Outline drawings of typical "solid" shapes are given on the second page. These need to be doubled in size to be on the same scale as the *Diplodocus*.

Use fairly thick sheet, then carve and round the cut out shapes to produce a more realistic model. Finish by painting in suitable colours, using poster colours or non-emulsion paints.

You can also use these outline drawings to prepare skeleton drawings of the animals, for making skeleton models like the *Diplodocus*. Study illustrations of the bones of the animal you wish to model, and complete your own skeleton drawing. Guesswork can help if you cannot find enough illustrations to follow, or, better still, take your sketchbook to a museum where you can see actual specimens.

As your skill grows, you can make more elaborate skeleton models, carving the pieces to correct bone shape from sheet balsa, rather than just using plain pieces.

Diplodocus: 100 ft. (30 m.) long

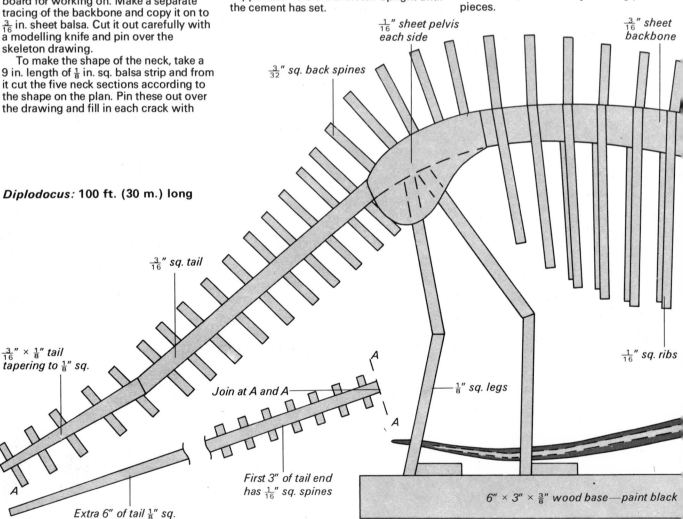

$\frac{1}{16}$" *sheet pelvis each side*

$\frac{3}{16}$" *sheet backbone*

$\frac{3}{32}$" *sq. back spines*

$\frac{3}{16}$" *sq. tail*

$\frac{1}{16}$" *sq. ribs*

$\frac{3}{16}$" × $\frac{1}{8}$" *tail tapering to $\frac{1}{8}$" sq.*

Join at A and A

$\frac{1}{8}$" *sq. legs*

First 3" of tail end has $\frac{1}{16}$" sq. spines

Extra 6" of tail $\frac{1}{8}$" sq.

6" × 3" × $\frac{3}{8}$" *wood base—paint black*

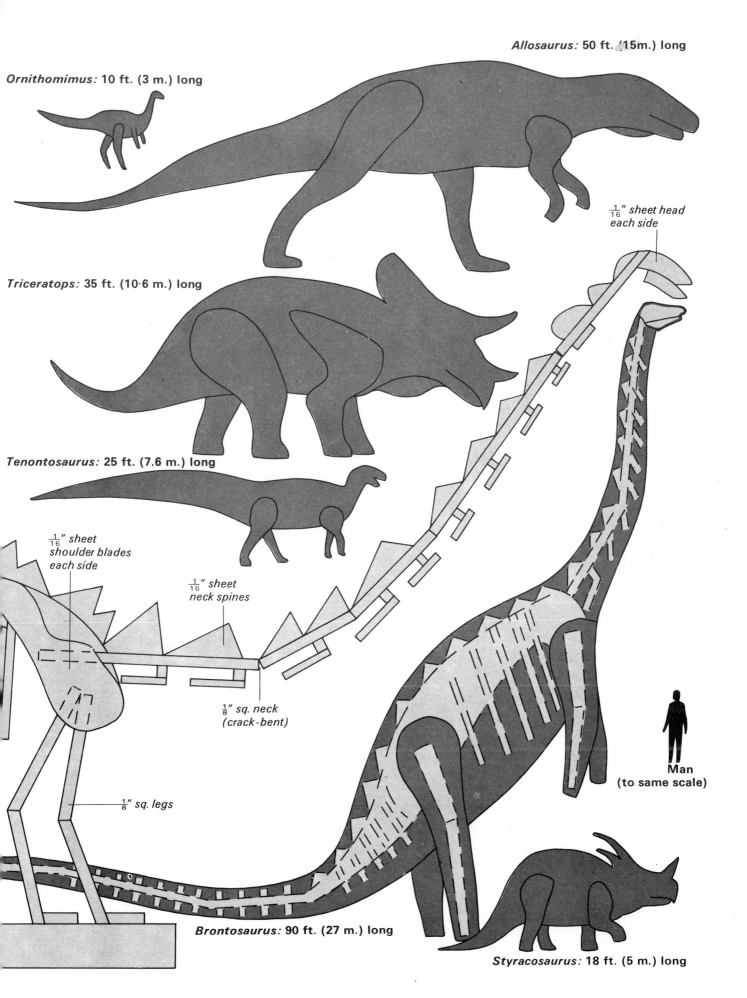

Ornithomimus: 10 ft. (3 m.) long

Allosaurus: 50 ft. (15m.) long

1/16" sheet head each side

Triceratops: 35 ft. (10·6 m.) long

Tenontosaurus: 25 ft. (7.6 m.) long

1/16" sheet shoulder blades each side

1/16" sheet neck spines

1/8" sq. neck (crack-bent)

1/8" sq. legs

Man (to same scale)

Brontosaurus: 90 ft. (27 m.) long

Styracosaurus: 18 ft. (5 m.) long

43

Projects fossils, pottery and painting

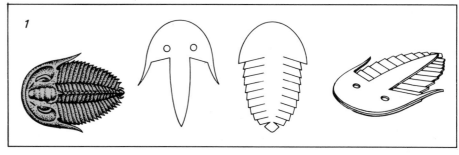

1

Early clay pots

The first containers man made were baskets, and an early clay pot found in Persia suggests that the first pots were made as imitation baskets.

To make a pot like those of early man you must first dig some clay and prepare it, then make your pot and fire it. Be sure to ask permission before digging clay. In the country you can find it on the banks of streams; in a city, ask the workmen on a building site for some. The colour of clay varies from grey to red, and you can easily tell it from ordinary dirt as it sticks together without crumbling when you squeeze it.

Dig the clay, making sure it is free from stones and leaves, and take it home in a plastic bag. Spread it out in a warm place to dry.

▲ When dry, break the clay into small pieces with a mallet. Sprinkle the pieces with water and when it has soaked in, work them into a ball with your hands, kneading it to get any air out. The clay should now feel like plasticine.

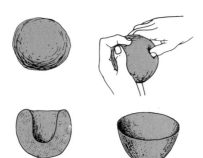

▲ Mix in sand equal to a quarter the amount of clay and roll the mixture into a ball. Work the mixture with your fingers into the shape of a pot. Scratch a design on your pot with a pencil or press marks into the clay with a seashell.

How fossils are formed

Trace the two shapes shown in Fig. 1 on to thick blotting paper, then cut out carefully with a modelling knife and make the slits. Lightly glue one piece on top of the other with ordinary gum and you have made a model trilobite.

Mould a large lump of plasticine into a rectangular block, about 3 in. × 2 in. and about half an inch deep. Carefully press your model trilobite down into

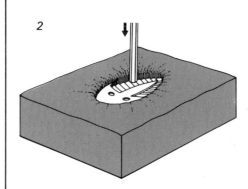

2

the centre of this with the end of a pencil, as shown in Fig. 2.

Make up a thin mixture of plaster of Paris and water. Using a small brush, paint this mixture on to the trilobite. Do not paint on any more than is necessary to soak the blotting paper model completely. If necessary, pour off surplus plaster by tipping the block on one side. Leave until the plaster has set hard, then cover with plasticine (Fig. 3).

3

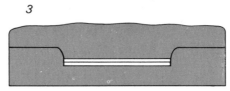

You have now transformed a soft "animal" (the blotting paper trilobite) into a hard fossil, buried in plasticine rock. This simple model shows one way in which fossils are formed. Their softish shell is replaced by hard silica (in this case plaster). The fossil will be disclosed by breaking away the plasticine, just as real fossils are found by chipping away rock.

Make another blotting paper trilobite. This time make a larger hollow in the plasticine block and fill with a stiff plaster of Paris and water mixture (Fig. 4). Press the trilobite model face down into the plaster and leave the plaster to set hard.

4

Place in the sink and pour boiling water on to the blotting paper model until the paper is soft and parts begin to wash away. Dry the top of the plaster surface carefully with cotton wool, and smear lightly with a little vaseline. Build a wall of plasticine around the top to act as a dam and fill this area with more plaster (Fig. 5). Leave until hard.

5

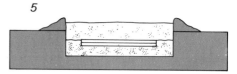

You have now made another type of fossil, where the original "animal" has dissolved away leaving an impression of its original shape in hard rock (the plaster). Break open the plaster to disclose this fossil impression (Fig. 6). The vaseline will make it easy to separate the top piece of plaster without breaking or cracking the fossil mould.

6

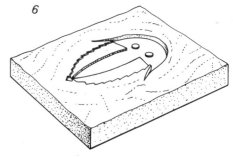

Make your own paints

Why not try making paints like those of early man? Collect heather or bilberries for the colour blue, dog daisy pollen for yellow, bramble leaves for green, parsley or mint for pale green, rose-hip or hawthorne berries for red, and black or red currants for purple.

Put the berries or leaves into a metal container and grind with a big stone. Then cover with water, using less water for berries. Mix with a stick. For brighter colours, boil the mixture slightly.

Experiment with other leaves and different kinds of earth for more interesting colours.

Use your home-made paints to experiment with prehistoric painting methods. Use a pad of fur or moss, a shredded twig and a feather to paint on rocks.

▲ Draw an outline of your picture on to the rock with the burnt end of a stick or pencil.

▲ Cover the rock with fat or wallpaper paste. Paste is better because fat smells.

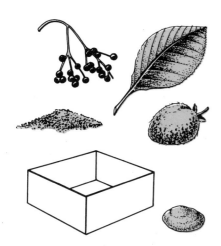

Blow painting

Prehistoric man would have used paints such as these for blow painting. But if you want to try blow painting it is easier and safer to use powdered paint.

Find a rock. Any size will do but it is more difficult to blow paint on to a small rock. Try to choose one with interesting shapes so that you can use the shape to add dimensions to your painting.

▲ Put a teaspoonful of powdered paint onto one end of a straw. Blow gently through the other end, in a straight line, at the rock.

More project ideas

The study of prehistoric life suggests many projects. Here are some which you might try.

Prehistoric man's resources

Prehistoric man had only the natural materials at hand to use for food, clothing and shelter. If you had to be either a foodgatherer or a hunter, what could you find in the country-side today? Make a typical menu for a prehistoric man's meal and compare it with one today.

What kind of shelter could you construct and what things should you consider about the site you choose for your prehistoric home?

Reptile wall chart

Make a wall chart showing reptiles of today. Concentrate on lizards that look rather like dinosaurs. Point out any interesting likenesses or differences between the reptiles of today and the dinosaurs.

Creation of the earth

There are many different stories and legends about the creation of the earth and life. Try to find out about some of them and make them up into an illustrated scrap-book.

Collecting fossils

The tools you need for fossil collecting are a geologist's hammer (a 16 oz. tinman's hammer will do instead), a cold chisel, a box of tissues for wrapping specimens in and a satchel or rucksack for carrying them home. A pair of goggles, or sunglasses, should be added to your kit to protect your eyes from flying chips of rock when digging out specimens.

To know where to look for fossils you will need expert advice. Ask your local museum. They will know if nearby rocks are likely to contain fossils, and where you can go to try your luck. Some fossils are still to be found in the open: usually on rocky beaches, down by the water's edge at low tide. But you will have to dig most of them out of fossil-bearing rocks.

When digging, always cut out a complete chunk of rock containing the fossil. Never try to chisel the fossil out of the rock as you will only break it to pieces. You may be able to separate the fossil later by very careful and patient work at home.

The chart on the left will help you to find out how old your fossils are.

ROCK AGES AND FOSSILS	
Cambrian and Ordovician	Brachiopods, gastropods, graptolites and trilobites
Silurian	Brachiopods, cephalopods, graptolites and trilobites
Devonian	Goniatites
Carboniferous	Brachiopods, corals and goniatites
Triassic	Ammonites
Jurassic	Ammonites and brachiopods
Cretaceous	Ammonites, brachiopods and urchins
Tertiary	Gastropods and nummulites

Reference

Places to Visit

British Museum (Natural History), London.
Geological Museum, London.
University Museum, Oxford.
Field Museum of Natural History, Chicago.
American Museum of Natural History, New York.

Suggested reading

Creation
How Life Began *by Irving Adler (Dobson)*.

Fish
The Fishes *by F. D. Ommanney (Time-Life)*.

Birds
Fossil Birds *by W. E. Swinton (British Museum)*.

Dinosaurs
The Dinosaurs *by W. E. Swinton (British Museum)*.
Fossil Amphibians and Reptiles *by W. E. Swinton (British Museum)*.
Dinosaurs and Other Prehistoric Animals *by Alfred Leutscher (Hamlyn, paperback Cox)*.
Dinosaurs and Other Prehistoric Reptiles *by Jane Wener Watson (Hamlyn)*.
Prehistoric Animals *by Vernon Mills (Purnell)*.
The Age of the Dinosaurs *by Bjorn Kurten (Weidenfeld and Nicolson)*.

Mammals
Prehistoric Mammals *by Martin L. Keen (Transworld)*.

Man
Early Man *by F. Clark Howell (Time-Life)*.
The History of Man *by Carleton S. Coon (Penguin)*.
From Ape to Adam *by Herbert Wendt (Thames and Hudson)*.
The Stone Age Hunters *by Grahame Clark (Thames and Hudson)*.

Everyday Life in Prehistoric Times; The New Stone Age *by Marjorie and C. H. B. Quennell (Transworld)*.
Everyday Life in Prehistoric Times; The Old Stone Age *by Marjorie and C. H. B. Quennell (Transworld)*.
Fossil Man *by Michael Day (Hamlyn)*.
Making Fire and Lightning *by W. T. O'Dea (Her Majesty's Stationery Office, The Science Museum)*.
We Are Not the First *by Andrew Tomas (Sphere)*.
The Origins of Man *by John Napier (Bodley Head)*.
Chariots of the Gods *by Erich Von Daniken (Corgi)*.
Return to the Stars *by Erich Von Daniken (Corgi)*.

How Do We Know?
Prehistory *by Derek Roe (Paladin)*.

Story in Stone
Fossils *by Rhodes and Zim (Hamlyn)*.

Mistaken Identity
See under general.

Darwin
Evolution *by Ruth Moore (Time-Life)*.

Survivors
Big Foot *by John Napier (Jonathan Cape)*.

Geological Eras
The Earth *by Arthur Beiser (Time-Life)*.

General Reading on Prehistoric Life
A Guide to Earth History *by Richard Carrington (Penguin)*.
Prehistoric Life on Earth *by Kai Peterson (Methuen)*.
Man and the Vertebrates *by A. S. Romer (Penguin)*.
Before the Deluge *by Herbert Wendt (Gollancz)*.
Life before Man *by Zdenek W. Spinar (Thames and Hudson)*.
The Succession of Life through Geological Time *by Kenneth P. Oakley and Helen M. Muir-Wood (British Museum)*.
Fun with Palaeontology *by William C. Cartner (Kaye & Ward)*.
The Dawn of Life *by Giovanni Pinna (Orbis)*.

GLOSSARY

aestivation to spend a warm and/or dry period in a state of stupor.

arboreal adapted for living in the trees.

archaeopteryx to date the oldest known type of bird.

carnivorous flesh eating.

cold-blooded having a body temperature that varies with the surroundings (e.g. reptile).

diurnal active during the day.

herbivorous plant eating.

invertebrate not having a backbone.

non vascular not provided with vessels or ducts for moving fluids.

nutrient something which nourishes.

organism a living thing.

percussion striking of one object against another.

photosynthesis by using sunlight as a source of energy the plant produces organic substances, especially sugar.

prehistory the period before recorded history.

protist(a) single-celled organism, either plant or animal.

transitional changing from one condition to another.

vascular provided with vessels or ducts for moving fluids.

vertebrate having a backbone or spinal column.

warm-blooded having a body temperature that is relatively constant (e.g. mammal).

Index

Illustration Credits
Key to the positions of illustrations: (T) top, (C) centre, (B) bottom and combinations; for example (TR) top right, or (CL) centre left.

Artists
Eric Jewell Associates Limited: 3, 10(B), 11(B), 32–33
Tudor Art Agency Limited: 4–5
Peter Connolly: 6–7, 8–9, 10(T), 11(T), 12–13, 14–15, 20–21, 22–23, 30(TL)(BTL), 38–39
John Shackle: 18–19
Tessa Jordan: 24–25, 28–29
The Garden Studio/Fred Anderson: 26–27
Ruth Brown: 30 (except TL and C), 31
Colin Rose: 34–35, 40–41, 44–45
David Shackle: 42–43

Photographs
British Museum (Natural History): 11(TR), 31(TR)
Netherlands National Tourist Office: 16(T)
Barnabys Picture Library: 16(B), 17(B)
Crown Copyright, Ministry of Transport: 17(T)
Peak Park Planning Board: 17(C)
Australia News & Information Bureau: 22(BL) (BR)
United Press International Ltd: 24(C)
French Tourist Office: 29(BL)
Mansell Collection: 31(CR), 32(TL), 40(BL)
Wellcome Institute: 32(BL)
Imitor Ltd (Peter Green): 34–35, 36–37
Novosti Press Agency: 34(TR)
The Royal Society/Dr Adam Locket: 38(TR)(CTR)
New Zealand House: 38(CBR)
Keystone Press Agency: 39(T)